Images of

Hope

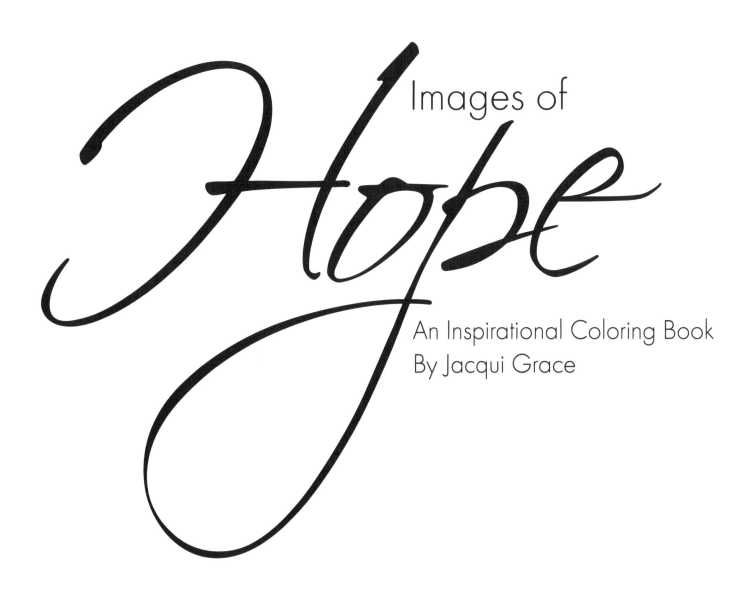

Images of Hope

An Inspirational Coloring Book
By Jacqui Grace

BETHANY HOUSE
a division of Baker Publishing Group
Minneapolis, Minnesota

Illustrations © 2016 by Jacqui Grace
Text © 2016 Just Cards Direct Limited

Published by Bethany House Publishers
11400 Hampshire Avenue South
Bloomington, Minnesota 55438
www.bethanyhouse.com

Bethany House Publishers is a division of
Baker Publishing Group, Grand Rapids, Michigan

Bethany House edition published 2016
ISBN 978-0-7642-1950-4

Previously published in the UK by Just Cards Publishing,
a division of Just Cards Direct Limited.

Printed in the United States of America

Graphic design by Emily Lee

16 17 18 19 20 21 22   7 6 5 4 3 2 1

Foreword

Following the huge success of her first inspirational coloring book, Jacqui Grace has now produced an amazing successor to *Images of Grace*.

Images of Hope contains beautiful hand-drawn illustrations, based on Scripture verses, each one thoughtful, original and brimming with hope.

Hope is a wonderful theme for a book. In recent weeks I have been considering the subject more deeply. I realize it is a basic human need, required by every individual on our planet—from kings to paupers, astronauts to street sweepers, we all need to know that there is something to hope for. Even in the darkest moments of our lives, when hope appears all but extinguished, it will eventually emerge again. Just as spring follows winter, ushering in new life once more, hope will return. We hope for many things—for food on the table, a better job, love, security, friends, and a home to call our own. Ultimately, our hopes and dreams are met in Christ—to a measure here on earth, but eternally with Him. I pray that you truly enjoy and are encouraged by this journey through *Hope*.

To inspire you on this journey, we have gathered together a few testimonies from people who have enjoyed Jacqui's first book, *Images of Grace*:

"It's hard to overstate how much I love *Images of Grace*—it's quickly becoming my favorite way to relax and reflect during the busy week. Coloring the Scriptures helps me rest and connect with God in new ways, and I always have encouraging verses floating round my head!"

Jo, Crawley, UK

"I love the simplicity and innocence of this coloring book. God fills me with childlike wonder and excitement as I turn each page. Thank you!"

Jacqui, Surrey, UK

"*Images of Grace* allows me to meditate on the Scriptures and provides an outlet for my creativity, all without taking up too much time, which is important to me as the mother of a one year old."

Tracy, Guildford, UK

"I love this coloring book—it is very inspiring to color. When you read the verses it makes you think and color in a different way than with an ordinary coloring book."

Alie, Kampen, The Netherlands

"*Images of Grace* is so amazing—it has really helped me keep my day focused on God."

Myranda, Minnesota, USA

Anne Horrobin
Director
Just Cards Direct
www.justcardsdirect.com

Introduction

For me, the "coloring book adventure" was unexpected and began in a surprising way. A little while ago, I damaged my hand through doing too much repetitive and intricate stitching and as a result I was forced to take a rest. This opened up valuable time to think, to reassess and to seek God for His plans for me.

It was also a chance to revisit old dreams and ideas and to remember the things that first inspired and motivated me. One of the things that has always enthralled me is Scripture. God's Word contains so many wise and wonderful truths, and as I dwelt on them, I began to doodle—and those doodles were the beginnings of the book you're holding today and the start of a new and exciting chapter in my life!

I strongly believe that because we are created in the image of Creator God, we each have creativity placed within us. It might be music, gardening, dancing, knitting or woodwork...

the list is long and diverse. Childhood often provides the freedom and opportunity to explore this creativity, but the busyness and complexity of adult life can sometimes leave little space for such things.

My prayer is that this book will remind you of the simple delight of creating, and also of those dreams and ideas that may have been long forgotten. I hope that it will inspire you to explore your own creativity, the things that you love doing and the things that you were created to do. Most of all, I pray that it would help you to take time out to draw closer to Creator God and to discover the amazing plans that He has for your life.

How to use this book

Coloring is relaxing and therapeutic—it helps us unwind, provides space to help us think and gives us an opportunity to enjoy the simple pleasures that color and creativity bring. As we carve out a moment or two in our busy lives to allow God to speak through creativity, He moves powerfully in our lives.

There is no right or wrong way to use this book, but here are a few suggestions to get you started:

- You don't have to start at the beginning, just pick a page that appeals to you.

- Colored pencils will give you the best results and allow you to blend and shade your colors. Fine-tipped felt pens will work well too, but test a small corner first to make sure that they don't bleed through the page.

- As you color, think about the words and meditate on them. Does anything in particular stand out to you? Why? Allow God to speak to you as you color.

- Maybe you could commit some of the verses to memory? Or look up the verses in different translations and explore the passage in more depth.

- Some of the pages have no words. Perhaps you could use these as a way of praying for different people or situations, or of working through your own thoughts and ideas.

- Don't be shy to share your creations and what you've learned. Show a friend, frame it, stick it on your fridge or share it on social media. We'd love to see your work and hear your stories—please do share them on the Just Cards Direct pages on Facebook, Twitter, Pinterest or Instagram.

- Most of all, relax and have fun! Enjoy the process—not just the end result. Make this book your own individual expression of creativity.

Jacqui Grace

He has sent Me
to heal the brokenhearted,
To proclaim liberty to the captives,
And the opening of the prison
to those who are bound

Isaiah 61:1 (NKJV)

Beauty for Ashes
The Oil of Joy for Mourning
the Garment of Praise
for the Spirit of Heaviness

Isaiah 61v3 KJV

We have an anchor that keeps the soul, steadfast and sure while the billows roll

Fastened to the Rock which cannot move, grounded firm and deep in the Savior's love

Hymn by Priscilla J. Owens, 1882.

WINTER is Past... the TIME of SINGING Has Come

SONG OF SOLOMON 2v11+12 (esv)

You will show me the path of life; In Your presence is fullness of joy

Psalm 16:11 (NKJV)

I am thankful for....

GiVE

THANKS

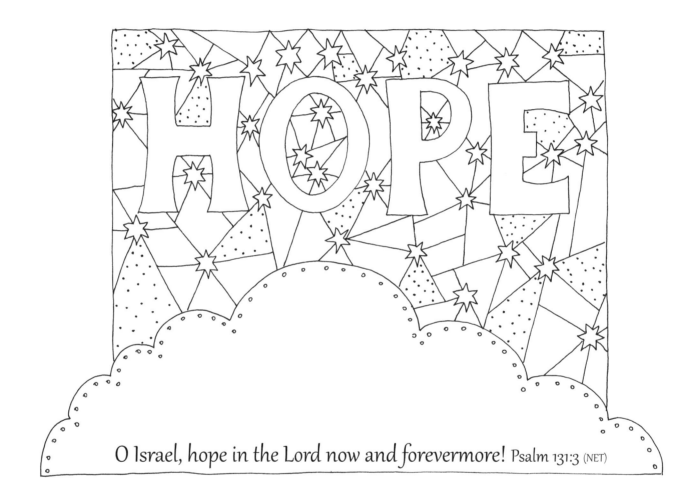

O Israel, hope in the Lord now and forevermore! Psalm 131:3 (NET)

HOPE IN the LORD now and evermore

Psalm 131 v 3 NET

Hymn written by Edwin Hatch 1878

God is able to do exceedingly, abundantly above all we ASK or IMAGINE

Ephesians 3:20

"I know the plans I have for you, declares the Lord."

plans TO GIVE YOU a FUTURE AND A HOPE

Jeremiah 29 v11 (ESV)

Created
to be
Creative

Whatever you do, do everything for the GLORY of GOD

1.Cor 10:31 NET

A time for everything

For everything
there is a season and
a time for every matter
under heaven

ECCLESIASTES 3:1 (ESV)

and the darkness HAS NOT Overcome IT

John 1v5 (ESV)

I say 'You are my God'

I trust in You, O Lord

My times are in Your hand.

Psalm 31 verse 14-15 esv

"*Lord God,*
it is you who have
made the heavens and
the earth by your great power...
Nothing is too hard for you"
Jeremiah 32:17 (esv)

Entreat me not to leave you, or to turn back from following after you; For WHEREVER YOU GO

I WILL GO

And wherever you lodge, I will lodge; Your people shall be my people, AND YOUR GOD, MY GOD.

Ruth 1:16 (NKJV)

the Kingdom of Heaven is like a mustard seed

matthew 13v31-32

I am fearfully and wonderfully made

Ps.139v14

Beautiful

loved

amazing

Individual

UNIQUE

Special

If God cares for the Birds,

how much more will He care for you?

Do not BE afraid

you are more VALUABLE than MANY sparrows

Matt 10:31 Net

He who *dwells* in the shelter of the Most High will *Abide* in the shadow of the Almighty.

I will say to the Lord, **"My refuge & my fortress,** my God, in whom I trust."

Psalm 91:1-2 (ESV)

Praise Him for all that is Past, and Praise Him for all that is past.

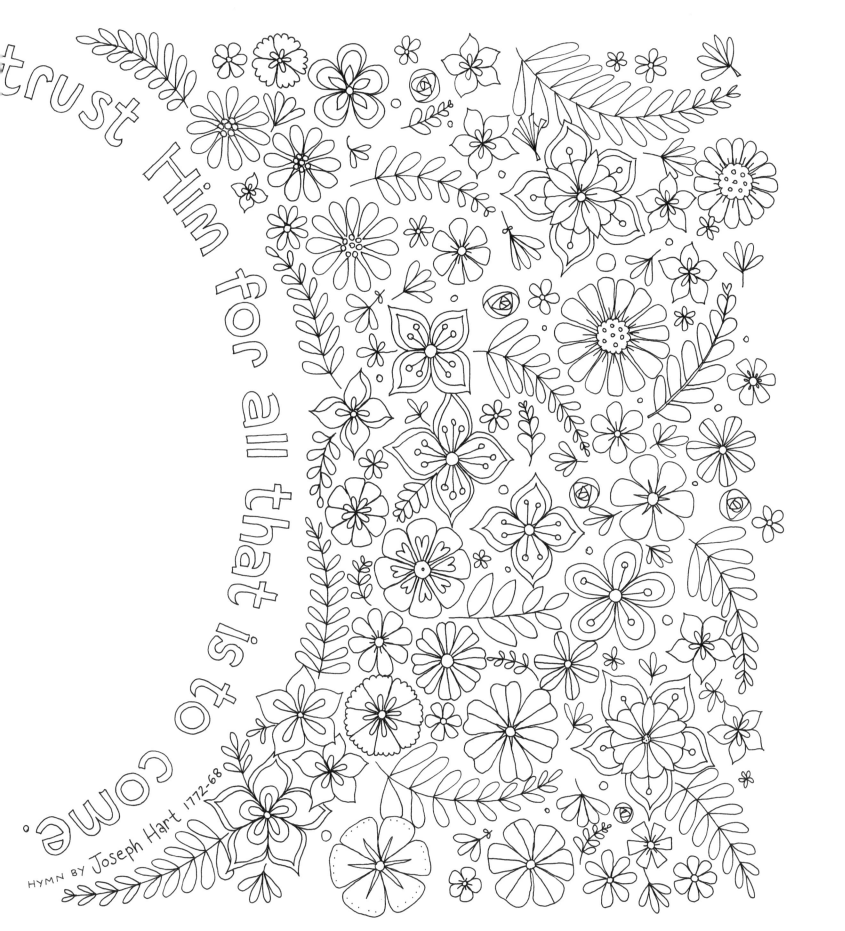

trust Him for all that is to come.

HYMN BY Joseph Hart 1772-68

Taste &
see that the
Lord is good

Psalm 34:8 (ESV)

SEEK THE LORD and HIS strength SEEK HIS face continually.

1 CHRON. 16 v 11

KJV

Now faith is the substance of things
hoped for, the evidence of things not seen.

Hebrews 11:1 (KJV)

faith is the substance of things hoped for, the EVIDENCE OF things NOT seen

Hebrews 11 v 1 KJV

Wait patiently; for it will certainly come to pass—it will not arrive late.

Habakkuk 2:3 (NET)

For God so loved the world that He gave His only begotten Son

John 3:16 (KJV)

the Desert shall rejoice and blossom...

Isaiah 35

THE Wilderness ... Shall BE Glad

honest

just

true

excellent

PURE

...think about these things

Philippians 4:8

from everlasting TO everlasting

Ps. 103:17
ESV

Even the WIND and the Sea OBEY HIM

peace

be still

Mark 4 v 39 + 41
KJV

My Pages

Have you got a favorite Bible verse or quote? If so, why not have a go at illustrating it on the following pages? Here are some simple steps to help you to create your own picture:

- Initially use a scrap piece of paper—this gives you the freedom to experiment, without any pressure. Alternatively, use the space below.

- Start by praying and then reading the quote slowly, dwelling on each individual word and noting if any particular word stands out.

- What is it about these words that you're drawn to? What is God saying?

- Do any images or experiences come to mind? Jot them down—be brave and experiment with ideas on your piece of paper.

- When you're ready, begin by writing your quote (lightly) in pencil in your book.

- Once you're happy with the layout, draw over the pencil lines with a fine-tipped pen, erasing the pencil afterwards. Alternatively, you could print out the words on a computer, cut them out and stick them in.

- Look back at the thoughts and pictures you jotted down at the beginning, and, using them for inspiration, begin to draw in and around your words.

- And finally, add some color! Enjoy yourself and allow God to speak to you.

Note: You might want to try this with a group, encouraging each other in your creativity and faith. It would work just as well in a Bible study or craft group as it would for personal meditation.

My Verse

My Doodles

Now try following the steps above to create your own pictures!

At Just Cards Direct, we are passionate about high quality inspirational design-led cards, gifts and books. We design many of our products ourselves, but also do source beautiful craft products from Africa, but either way the same sense of quality and design runs throughout. You can find out more at **www.justcardsdirect.com**.

In 2015 we launched our inspirational hand-drawn coloring books through Just Cards Publishing. For more information about us and our other publications please visit **www.justcardspublishing.com**.

Images of Hope is our 2nd inspirational coloring book, following on from the huge success of our 1st book, Images of Grace, both by Jacqui Grace. In the coming months we will be releasing a calendar, journals and an artist's edition of the book, all based on the artwork from the coloring books.

We would love to connect with you through social media—please do share your pictures and ideas with us on Facebook, Twitter, Pinterest or Instagram. Thank you!

Can't Get Enough Coloring? Enjoy More Hours of Fun and Inspiration With *Images of Grace*!

Blending intricate, hand-drawn illustrations with the rich words of Scripture, this exquisite coloring book is a gentle tonic for the busyness of life. Each page is a source of inspiration, giving you the opportunity to meditate on God's love for you as you color. Be inspired and amazed by grace!

BETHANY HOUSE

 Stay up to date on your favorite books and authors with our free e-newsletters. Sign up today at bethanyhouse.com.

 Find us on Facebook. facebook.com/BHPnonfiction

 Follow us on Twitter. @bethany_house